DK SUPER Planet

Wonderful Waterways

Dive in and explore our planet's incredible range of waterways, from rivers and canals to lakes and the great open oceans

DK

DK | Penguin Random House

Produced for DK by
Editorial Just Content Limited
Design Studio Noel

Author Steve Tomecek

Senior Editor Ankita Awasthi Tröger
Project Editor Amanda Eisenthal
Senior Art Editor Gilda Pacitti
Managing Editor Carine Tracanelli
Managing Art Editor Sarah Corcoran
Production Editor Jaypal Chauhan
DTP Designer Rohit Singh
Production Controller Rebecca Parton
Publisher Sarah Forbes
Managing Director, Learning Hilary Fine

First American Edition, 2025
Published in the United States by DK Publishing,
a division of Penguin Random House LLC
1745 Broadway, 20th Floor, New York, NY 10019

Copyright © 2025 Dorling Kindersley Limited
25 26 27 28 29 10 9 8 7 6 5 4 3 2 1
001–345275–Apr/2025

All rights reserved.
Without limiting the rights under the copyright reserved above, no part of this publication may be reproduced, stored in or introduced into a retrieval system, or transmitted, in any form, or by any means (electronic, mechanical, photocopying, recording, or otherwise), without the prior written permission of the copyright owner.
Published in Great Britain by Dorling Kindersley Limited

A catalog record for this book
is available from the Library of Congress.
HC ISBN: 978-0-5939-6252-7
PB ISBN: 978-0-5939-6251-0

DK books are available at special discounts when purchased in bulk for sales promotions, premiums, fund-raising, or educational use.
For details, contact: DK Publishing Special Markets,
1745 Broadway, 20th Floor, New York, NY 10019
SpecialSales@dk.com

Printed and bound in China

www.dk.com

This book was made with Forest Stewardship Council™ certified paper – one small step in DK's commitment to a sustainable future.
Learn more at www.dk.com/uk/information/sustainability

Contents

Water Wanderers	4
What is Water?	6
The Water Cycle	8
Dive into the Oceans	10
Explore the Beach	12
Look at Lakes	14
Famous Lakes	16
Tour the Great Lakes	18
Ride the Rivers	20
Famous Rivers	22
Delve into Dams	24
Amazing Waterfalls	26
Life by the Water	28
Waterside Habitats	30
Trading Places	32
Water Dangers	34
Everyday Science: Water in Space?	36
Let's Experiment! Make a Dam	38
Let's Experiment! Sink or Swim?	40
Vocabulary Builder: As the River Flows	42
Glossary	44
Index	46

Words in **bold** are explained in the glossary on page 44.

Water Wanderers

If you look at our planet, what do you see? That's right! It is mostly blue. This is because our planet is largely water. Most of this water is in the **ocean**. The rest can be found in different waterways, like **lakes**, **rivers**, and even underground.

Wet climates, like the rainforest, have a lot of rainfall. Dry climates, like the desert, have very little rainfall. All plants and animals need water to survive. So, it is important that we save water whenever we can.

Only a tiny amount of Earth's **fresh water** is found on Earth's surface. Many lakes, like the five Great Lakes, contain fresh water.

A hurricane is a storm that develops over the ocean. Water in the air helps create extreme weather conditions like hurricanes and tropical storms.

The Atacama Desert in Chile is one of the driest places on Earth. Some areas get less than 0.2 inches (5 mm) of rain a year.

Earth's water can be liquid or ice. **Glaciers** are large masses of ice. They hold three-quarters of Earth's fresh water. Global warming means many glaciers are melting. As glaciers melt, **sea** levels rise.

Rivers like the Amazon are important waterways. When it rains, the rainwater **flows** from mountains into rivers and finally to the ocean.

Tropical rainforests, like the Amazon in South America, have lots of rainfall. All of this water supports a huge variety of plants and animals.

71%

of Earth's surface is water, but very little can be used by humans as it is either too salty or solid ice.

Scientists estimate that Earth contains enough water to fill over

550 trillion

Olympic-sized swimming pools!

Around

97%

of Earth's water is in the oceans. The Pacific Ocean holds over half of the free water on Earth.

What is Water?

All living things need water to survive. Animals need water to drink. Plants need water to grow. But not all water on Earth is liquid. Water, like most matter, has three states: solid, liquid, and gas. Each state of water has different properties that cause it to act in different ways.

LIQUID WATER

Most water on Earth is found in the form of liquid water. Liquids flow easily and take the shape of the container they are placed in.

WATER VAPOR

When you heat water in a tea kettle, steam comes out. This steam is **water vapor**. When water evaporates, it turns into water vapor that rises up into the air.

SOLID ICE

Water is found in its solid form when it gets very cold. Most of the fresh water on Earth is in the form of ice, like huge glaciers.

Without water, there would be no life.

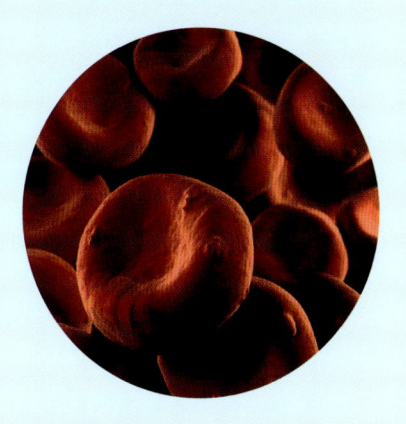

Your blood is made up of many tiny cells. They flow in a liquid called plasma. Plasma is over

90% water.

Maple syrup is made from tree sap. Sap carries water and food through the tree. It is mostly water.

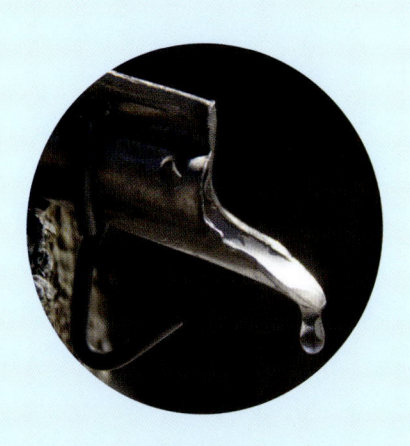

The Water Cycle

Earth is mostly covered by water. All this water moves through the land, oceans, and **atmosphere** over and over again. This is known as the water cycle. As water moves through the water cycle, it can be liquid, solid, or gas.

2 When water vapor in the air cools down and turns back into a liquid, it forms tiny drops of water in clouds. This is called **condensation**.

1 Energy from the Sun causes liquid water in lakes and oceans to turn into water vapor and rise into the air. This is called **evaporation**.

Fascinating fact

Scientists believe that Earth's water first formed in space 4.5 billion years ago. Some of this water might be as old as the Sun!

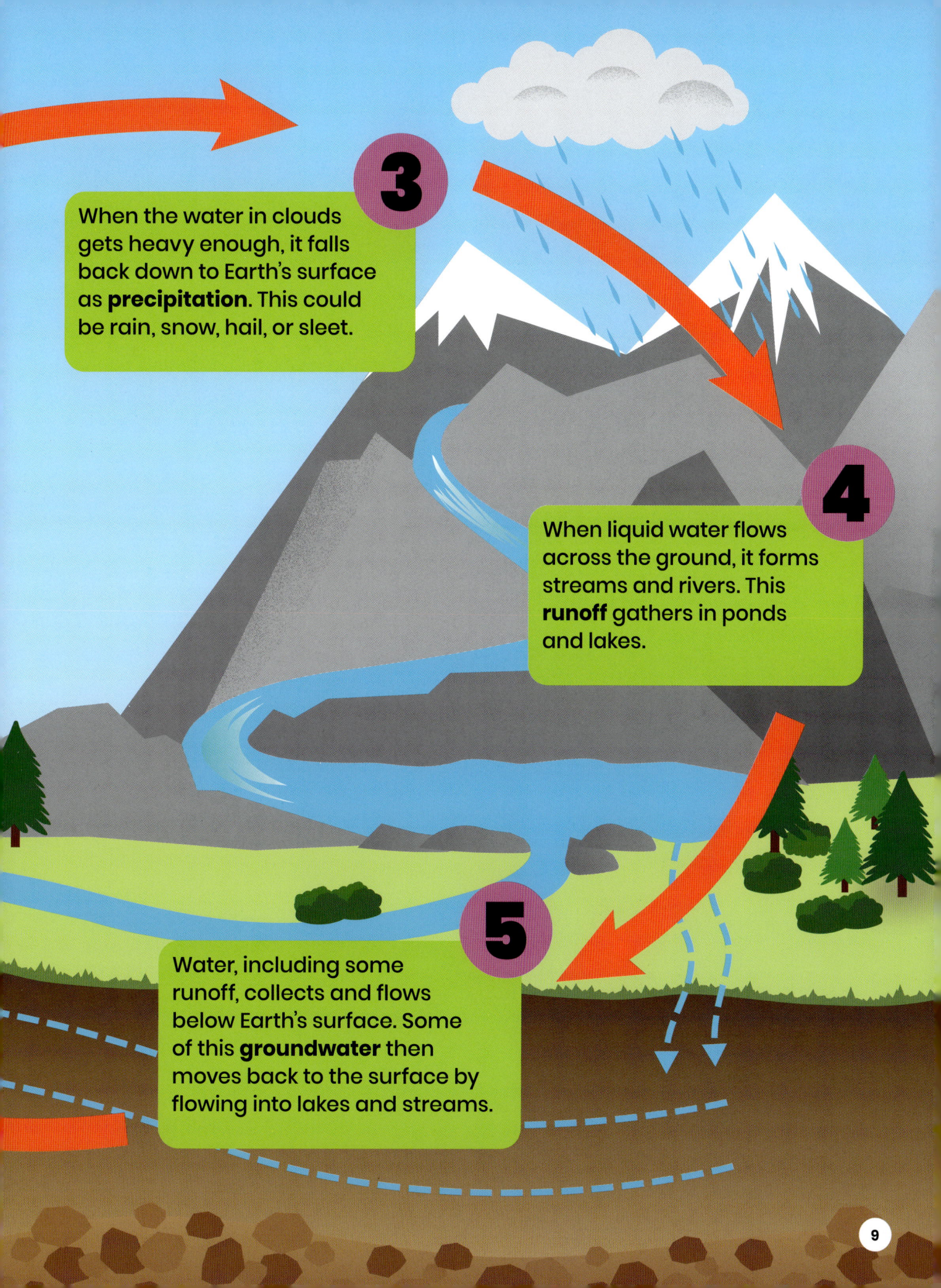

3 When the water in clouds gets heavy enough, it falls back down to Earth's surface as **precipitation**. This could be rain, snow, hail, or sleet.

4 When liquid water flows across the ground, it forms streams and rivers. This **runoff** gathers in ponds and lakes.

5 Water, including some runoff, collects and flows below Earth's surface. Some of this **groundwater** then moves back to the surface by flowing into lakes and streams.

Dive into the Oceans

Almost all of Earth's water is found in the ocean. Below the surface, oceans contain some incredible **habitats** that are home to many different creatures.

Find out!

Can you find out the names of three different mammals that live in the ocean?

There are many tens of thousands of different species of fish in the ocean. They range in size from tiny seahorses to huge whale sharks.

Many invertebrates—animals without a backbone—live in the ocean. This includes clams, crabs, and sea stars.

Ocean reefs are made by sea creatures called corals that live in large groups. As global warming heats Earth's oceans, many corals are dying and the reefs are turning white. This is called bleaching.

Whales are **mammals**. They come up to the surface to breathe air. Orcas usually spend just one to two minutes at a time underwater.

Not everything that is in the ocean belongs there. The Great Pacific Garbage Patch contains trillions of tiny pieces of plastic and other trash. Many people are working together to clean up our oceans.

Parts of the ocean

Scientists give special names to different parts of the ocean. These tell us where they are and what they look like.

GULF
This is a part of the ocean that goes a long way into the land. A **gulf** is surrounded by land on most sides with an opening to the sea.

SEA
This is smaller than an ocean and is the part of the ocean that is near the land.

BAY
This is a part of the ocean that goes into the land, like a gulf. **Bays** are not as deep or as enclosed as gulfs.

STRAIT
A **strait** is a narrow passage between land that connects two seas.

Explore the Beach

Broad, flat areas that can be found next to oceans, rivers, or lakes are called **beaches**. They can be sandy or covered in rocks or pebbles. An ocean beach is constantly shaped by waves. Beaches provide homes for many different plants and animals, including ones that live in tide pools.

Many ocean beaches have **cliffs** beside them. A cliff forms when waves crash into the shore, cutting into the land.

The **coast** is where the land meets the sea. Beaches are found along the coast.

Tide pools form when the **salt water** from the ocean washes onto the shore. The water forms a pool where different plants and animals live.

Sand **dunes** protect coasts and are very important for wildlife.

Find out!

Climate change is causing sea levels to rise, which can affect beaches. Can you find out some things people are doing to protect beaches?

Sea stars have hundreds of tiny tube feet that help them crawl along the ocean floor. Their mouth is in the centre of their lower surface, and they eat mussels and oysters.

Mussels have two hard shells that they can open and close. When they are in the water, they open their shells to eat.

Seaweed is a type of living thing called algae. It provides food and shelter for animals that live near the shore.

Sea urchins mostly eat algae. Many are covered with spiky spines. You don't want to step on them!

Hermit crabs live in the shells of other animals. When they outgrow their old shell, they find a bigger one.

Look at Lakes

Most of the water on Earth's surface is in the ocean. But large amounts of liquid water can also be found in lakes. A lake is a body of fresh water or salt water that is surrounded by land. Lakes are like bowls in the ground. They can also be found at the foot of mountains that rise around them.

Meltwater and runoff from rain collects in streams. They carry fresh water into the lake.

Some lakes have wetlands along their edges. Many animals and insects live in wetlands. The water can also flow back into the ground here.

People use lakes to sail, fish, and swim. **Docks** make it easier for people to get into the water and board ships.

Find out!

Are there any lakes in your area? What do people use the lakes for?

Water from snow and glaciers melts high in the mountains.

People can use fresh water from lakes for drinking water. The water can also be used for **irrigation**.

Lakes are also fed by groundwater, which is water that flows underground.

Saltwater lakes

Saltwater lakes form like freshwater lakes. Hot temperatures mean the water in the lake evaporates. The lake gets smaller and the water gets saltier. Over time, salt crusts can build up.

Animals like shrimp and worms can live in saltwater lakes. Birds often nest nearby as the lakes are a good source of food. However, the water is too salty to drink or use for irrigation.

Famous Lakes

You can find lakes on every continent on Earth. Here are six famous lakes around the world that are worth exploring.

LAKE BAIKAL

This is the deepest continental lake—it is over 1 mile (1.62 km) deep. This lake in Russia holds the most water of any freshwater lake on the planet and is home to the only freshwater seal species.

LAKE TITICACA

This is the largest freshwater lake in South America. It is the highest large lake in the world. People first settled here over three thousand years ago.

ARAL SEA

This is a saltwater lake in Central Asia that used to be huge. But people overused its water for irrigation and it dried up in the 2010s.

LAKE CHAD

This is a large freshwater lake that appears to be shrinking. This is a problem for the people who live around the lake and rely on it.

LAKE VICTORIA

This is the largest freshwater lake in Africa and the second largest on Earth. A large **dam** was built across one of the rivers leading out of the lake to make electricity. This made the lake even larger.

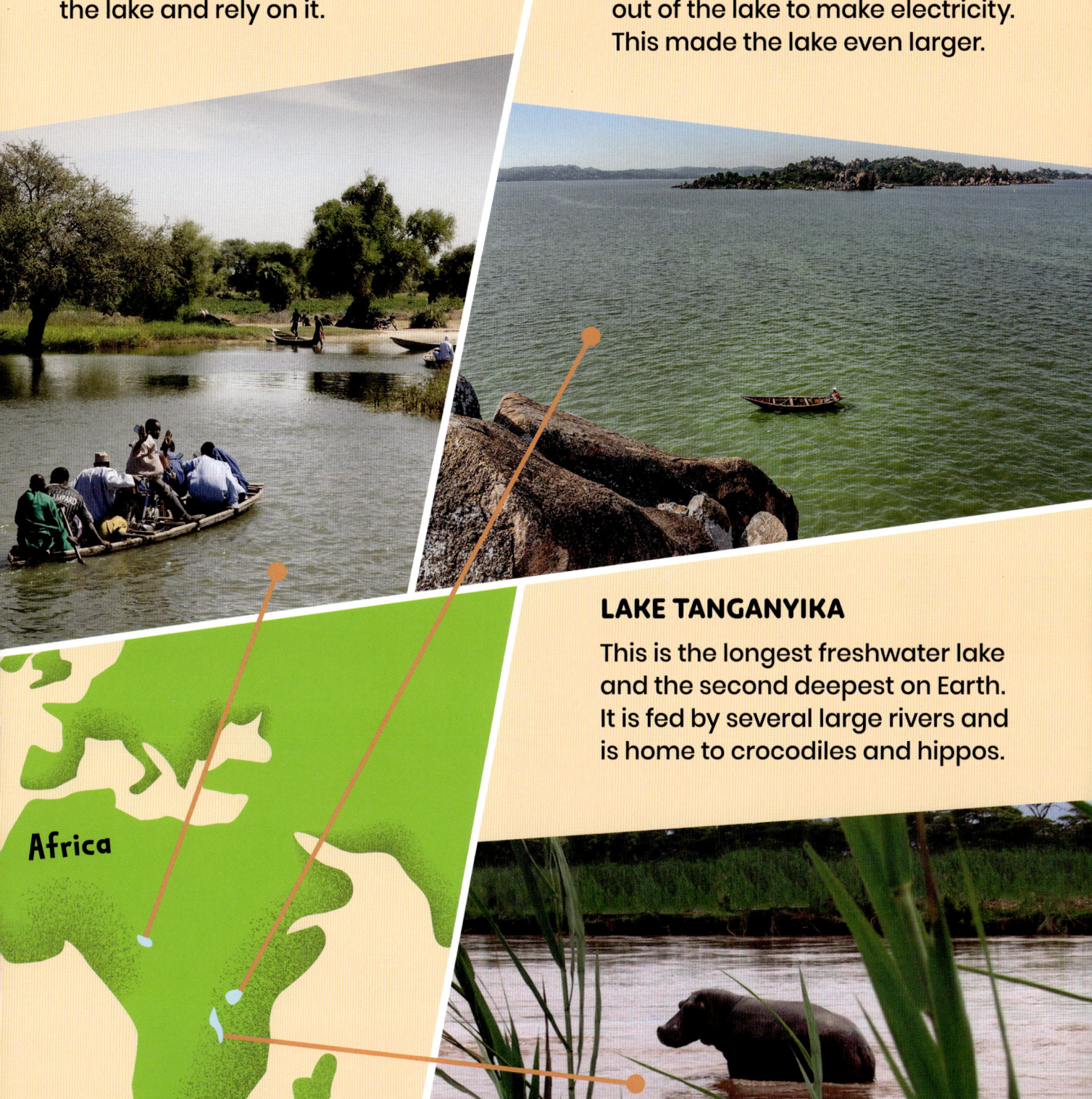

LAKE TANGANYIKA

This is the longest freshwater lake and the second deepest on Earth. It is fed by several large rivers and is home to crocodiles and hippos.

Africa

17

Tour the Great Lakes

The Great Lakes are in North America. They formed thousands of years ago when glaciers from the last ice age melted. The Great Lakes hold more than one-fifth of the Earth's fresh surface water. Over 30 million people depend on this water. The five lakes are connected and form a waterway over 750 miles (1,200 km) long. The lakes are important for wildlife, but pollution and shipping have caused problems. New laws have helped reduce these issues.

LAKE SUPERIOR

This is the largest and deepest of the Great Lakes. Because it is so deep, it does not completely freeze in winter. This is helpful for the many ships that sail on it.

LAKE HURON

There are over 30,000 islands in Lake Huron. The largest island is called Manitoulin Island. It has over 100 lakes.

LAKE MICHIGAN

This is the only lake entirely located in the US. Many large cities have developed on its shores, including Chicago (*above*) and Milwaukee.

Lake Superior

Canada

Lake Ontario

USA

Lake Huron

Lake Erie

Lake Michigan

LAKE ONTARIO

There are several **canals** connected to Lake Ontario. These were built so that large ships could enter the Great Lakes from the Atlantic Ocean.

LAKE ERIE

Ships transport goods between big industrial cities on the Great Lakes. Erie is the shallowest of the five lakes and freezes over during cold winters.

Ride the Rivers

1 The source of the river is where it starts.

All rivers are waterways. They often start at a **source** in the mountains and end at the sea in a **mouth**. Rivers provide water for drinking, transportation, and agriculture. There are thousands of rivers in the world, but they make up less than 1 percent of the surface water on Earth.

2 Rivers that flow through forests provide water, food, and a home for many mammals, including bears and beavers.

Find out!

Can you find out the name of a river in your area?

3 Wetlands are marshy areas along banks of slow-moving rivers. They are home to a variety of animals, including amphibians like frogs and salamanders, and reptiles like terrapins *(below)*.

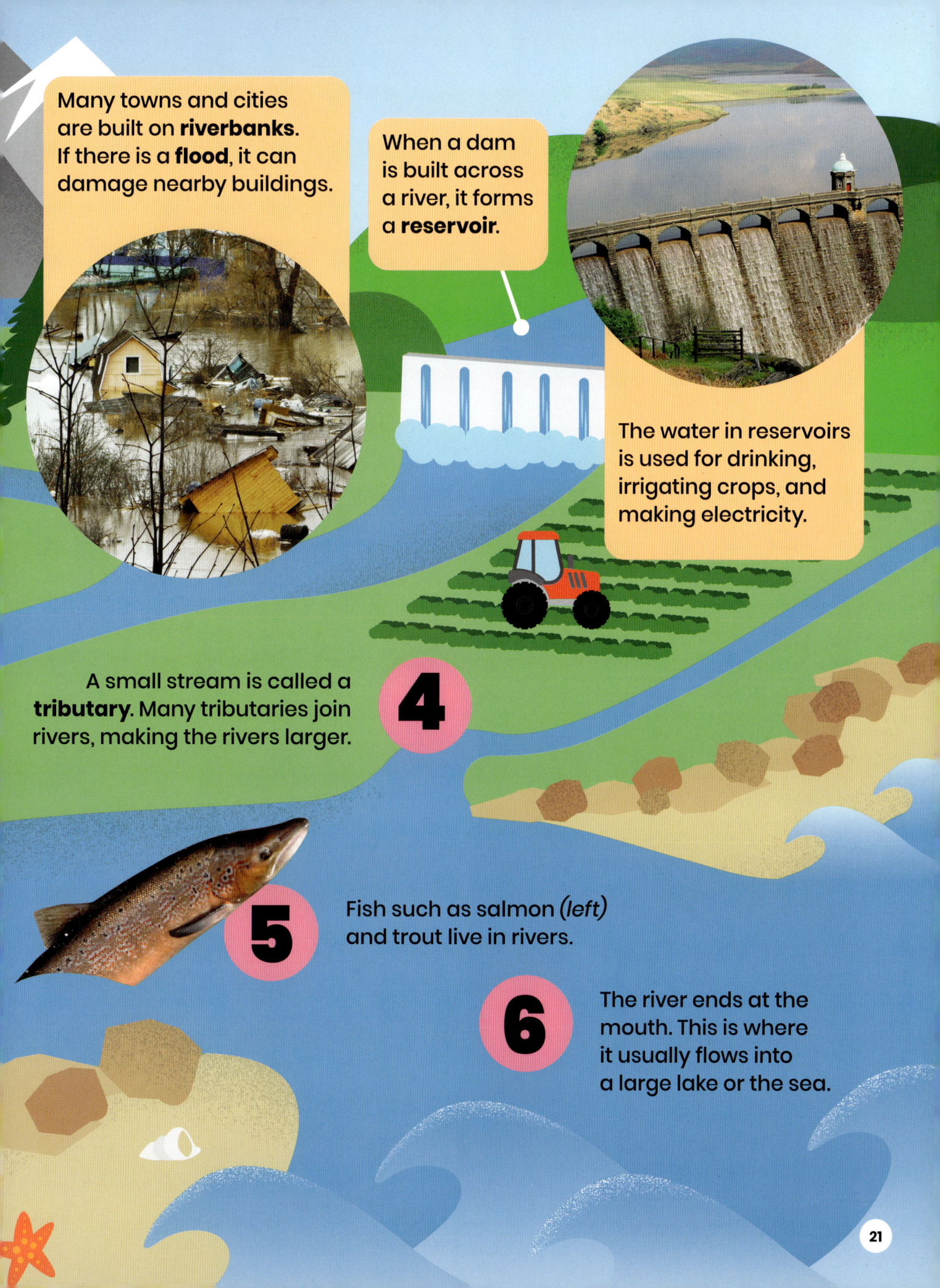

Many towns and cities are built on **riverbanks**. If there is a **flood**, it can damage nearby buildings.

When a dam is built across a river, it forms a **reservoir**.

The water in reservoirs is used for drinking, irrigating crops, and making electricity.

4 A small stream is called a **tributary**. Many tributaries join rivers, making the rivers larger.

5 Fish such as salmon (*left*) and trout live in rivers.

6 The river ends at the mouth. This is where it usually flows into a large lake or the sea.

21

Famous Rivers

Rivers provide an easy way to travel by boat, carry goods from one place to another, and irrigate crops. We will look at four famous rivers that have played an important role in the development of the areas where they are found.

HUÁNG HÉ (YELLOW RIVER)

This is known as "Mother River". Many of China's oldest cities can be found on its banks. The river has been used for farming since ancient times.

NILE RIVER

This is the longest river on Earth. Many **civilizations** have grown around the Nile River. Egyptians have used sailboats known as feluccas to transport goods since ancient times.

GANGES RIVER

This Indian river is sacred in the Hindu religion. Millions of people depend on the Ganges for drinking water and irrigation. As factories, farms, and sewers have emptied wastewater into the river, it has become very polluted. Work to clean up the river means that the numbers of dolphins and other wildlife in the river are increasing.

Fascinating fact

When people no longer needed paddle steamers, they left them on the riverbank. The Murray River is full of these shipwrecks.

MURRAY RIVER

This is the longest river in Australia. In the 19th century, people used paddle steamers to transport passengers and goods. Today, the river is an important source of water for drinking and farming.

Delve into Dams

People have been building dams for thousands of years to control water flow. A dam is like a wall that is built across a river. The wall creates a reservoir, or lake, behind it. Dams can have a big impact on the natural environment. People use dams to store water, prevent flooding, and make electricity.

RESERVOIR

This is an artificial lake that is formed behind a dam. The reservoir stores water.

SPILLWAY

This allows water to flow from the reservoir through the dam. If the reservoir gets too full, the spillway releases water to prevent flooding.

INTAKE TOWER

This is a structure that takes water from the reservoir using pipes. This allows the water to be used by people for drinking water and irrigation.

HYDROPOWER PLANT

This is a power plant that uses water from the dam to make electricity.

Fascinating fact

The oldest known dam is the Jawa Dam in Jordan, dating back to around 3000 BCE!

The Hoover Dam, in the US, has a huge hydropower plant that makes enough electricity to power a city.

The Aswan Dam is on the Nile River. Before the dam was built, the Nile would flood each year. Now, people can control the flooding.

The Kariba Dam is in southern Africa. Its reservoir is Lake Kariba. It holds more water than any other artificial lake in the world.

25

Amazing Waterfalls

They are dramatic sights. And they can roar like thunder. But if you are traveling by boat, waterfalls can make things difficult. Boats like white water rafts can go over smaller waterfalls. Getting a larger boat past a waterfall takes engineering—and a lot of digging.

Niagara Falls is located between Canada and the US. The Welland Canal was built to allow boats to go around the falls.

Find out!

Can you find out how high the highest waterfall on Earth is?

Salto Ángel (Angel Falls) in Venezuela is 3,211 ft (979 m) high.

Victoria Falls is located between Zambia and Zimbabwe. Victoria Falls is one of the few places on Earth where you can see a "moonbow". This is a rainbow that occurs at night under the light of a full moon.

White water rafts cannot go over bigger waterfalls. And if you need to transport goods or people, you need to **divert** the waterfall or go around it.

How locks work

Engineers build canals to allow boats to get around waterfalls. First they dig a side channel around the falls. Then they build a series of **locks** in the channel. A lock is like an elevator for boats. It is a section of the canal with big gates at each end. When a boat enters the lock, the gates close behind it. Water is added to raise the boat or removed to lower it. Once it is at the right level, the front gates open and the boat can go forward.

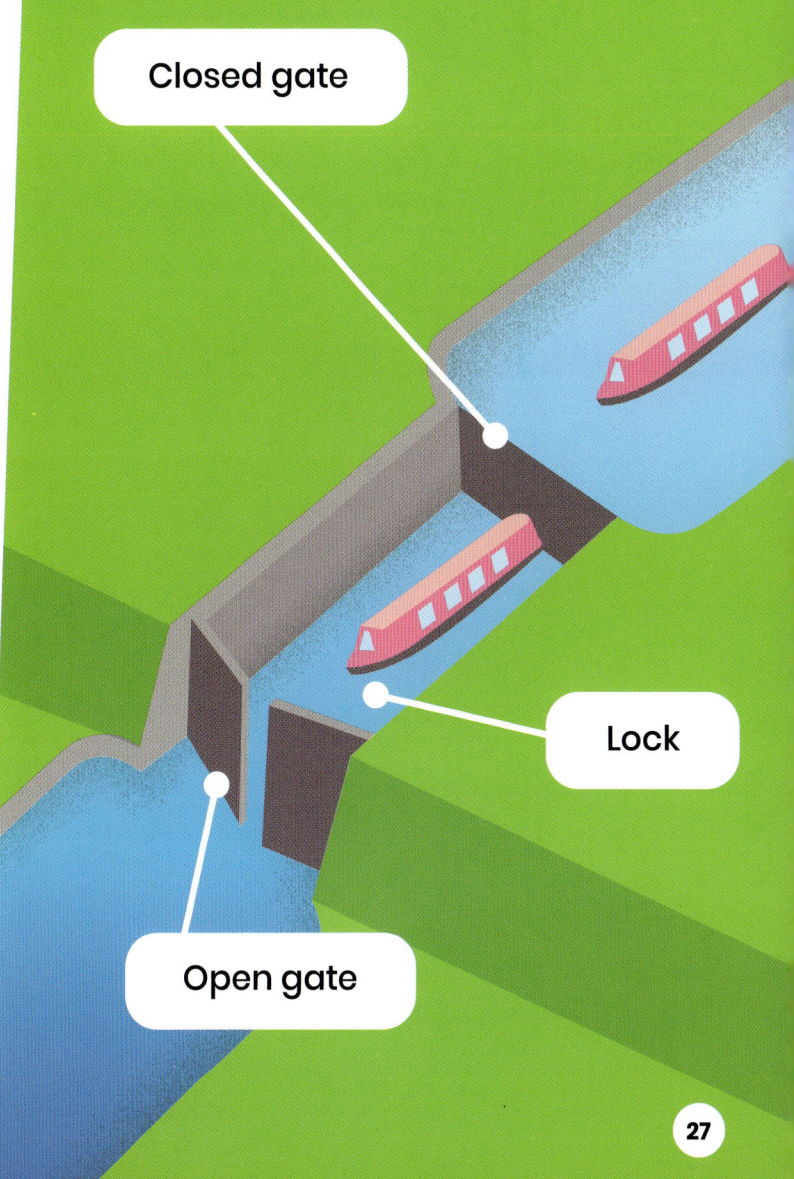

Closed gate

Lock

Open gate

Life by the Water

When people first started settling in towns and cities, they often chose places near waterways such as rivers. Rivers can provide a source of fresh drinking water, water for crops and animals, and a way to transport goods and people from one place to another.

IRRIGATION CANAL
This is a channel carrying water from the river to farm fields and **pastures**.

WATER INTAKE
This is where river water comes into the city. People use the water for drinking, cooking, and washing.

LEVEE
This is a wall or tall bank that stops river water from flooding the area around it.

DOCK
This is a structure built on the river. It allows people to ship goods and visit the city by boat.

FARM POND

This is where farm animals drink from. It is supplied by river water taken from a pipe or channel.

WASTEWATER TREATMENT PLANT

This is a place that cleans used water. The cleaned water goes back into the river.

Find out!

Can you find out the name of some cities built on rivers in your area?

Some of the oldest, biggest cities in the world were built on waterways. Cairo is on the Nile River in Egypt. Over 10 million people live there.

The city of Cape Town grew up next to Table Bay. It has 14 rivers and 10 wetlands and its harbour is one of South Africa's most important ports.

New Orleans is on the banks of the Mississippi River in the US. In 2005, Hurricane Katrina caused floods when water destroyed the levees that protect the city.

Waterside Habitats

Rivers and seashores create many different habitats for animals and plants to live. Some of the animals live in water. Others live on land. But they all depend on water to survive. Many different plants grow along the banks of waterways. These plants provide food and shelter for animals.

Otters *(left)*, herons *(right)*, and swallows *(above)* all depend on water for food and shelter.

Find out!

Can you find out more about a river near you? See if you can discover the names of one plant, one animal, and one fish that live there.

Big fish including bass (*above*), sturgeon, and catfish live in freshwater lakes.

Some trees, like willows, grow along riverbanks where the soil is wet.

Insects such as pond skaters (*above*) and dragonflies live and breed near ponds.

Ducks (*above*) and geese build their nests near water. They eat plants and animals in ponds, lakes, and rivers.

Frogs (*above*), salamanders, and snapping turtles live in and around ponds. They get their body heat from their environment.

Mangroves are tropical trees. They grow where fresh water from rivers enters the sea.

Water voles (*above*) and otters are mammals that live along riverbanks.

Birds like kingfishers (*above*) and herons hunt for fish in rivers and streams.

31

Trading Places

Since ancient times, rivers have formed important **transportation routes**. These routes allow people to easily move goods near and far.

Ports along the Mississippi River, like New Orleans, are important **trading hubs**. Goods move into and out of these ports from all over the world.

Fascinating fact

The Phoenicians established some of the earliest maritime trading routes around the 12th century BCE. They traded goods such as spices, glass, and purple dye.

In the past, goods were loaded and unloaded from ships and barges by hand. But thanks to modern technology, shipping containers can be moved easily between trucks, trains, and cargo ships.

32

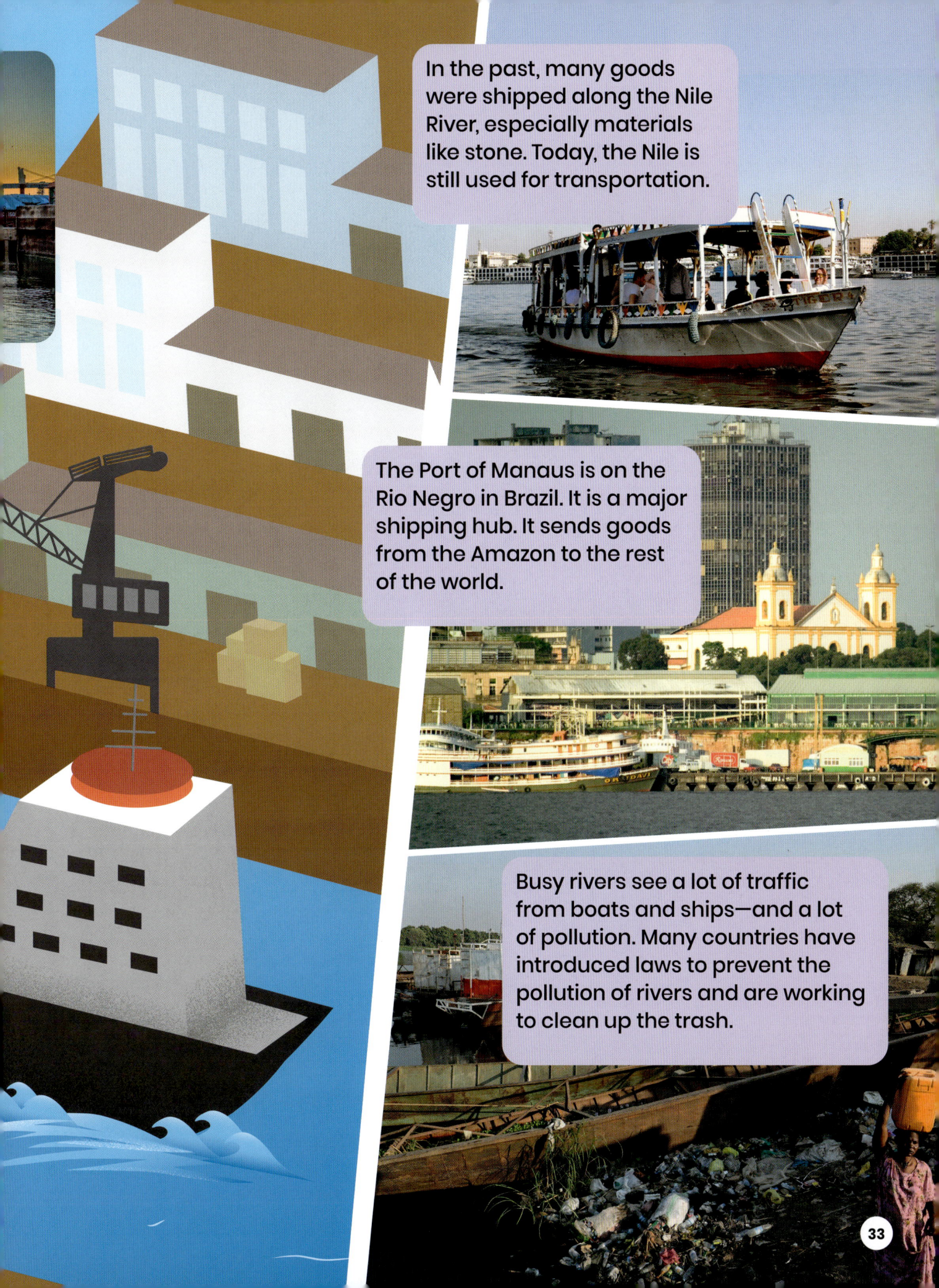

In the past, many goods were shipped along the Nile River, especially materials like stone. Today, the Nile is still used for transportation.

The Port of Manaus is on the Rio Negro in Brazil. It is a major shipping hub. It sends goods from the Amazon to the rest of the world.

Busy rivers see a lot of traffic from boats and ships—and a lot of pollution. Many countries have introduced laws to prevent the pollution of rivers and are working to clean up the trash.

33

Water Dangers

People have navigated rivers for thousands of years. It hasn't always been easy. There are many dangers in the water, like hidden rocks, fast-flowing **currents**, and **rapids**. Boat captains have to look out for these dangers so they can navigate them safely.

The Yangtze River in China is important for trade. Flood control measures have been used to help make it safer.

Rapids, large rocks, and fast-moving currents are very dangerous to boats.

Fascinating fact

In 1927, the Mississippi River in the US experienced a historic flood. This great flood submerged well over 23,000 sq miles (60,000 sq km) of land over several months.

The Ob River is in Russia. In the winter, parts of the river freeze. In the spring, melting snow can cause the icy river to flood. Boats can only travel on it part of the year.

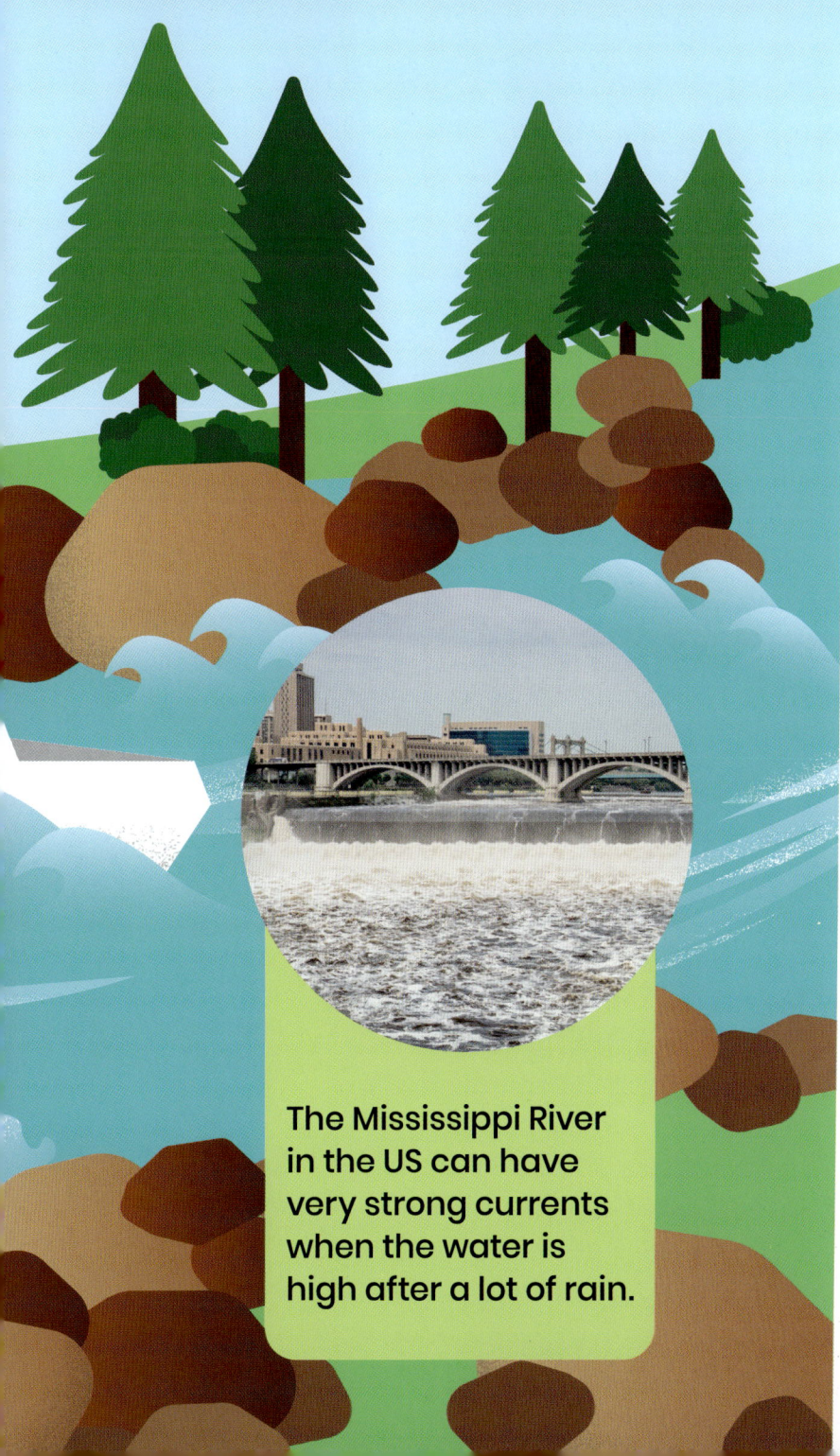

The Mississippi River in the US can have very strong currents when the water is high after a lot of rain.

Navigating safely

Currents on some rivers can be strong and unpredictable. Boat captains are trained to understand these currents and steer around them.

Today, boats use modern navigation equipment. Radar can tell a boat captain if there are rocks or other ships they might hit. GPS tells them exactly where the boat is.

35

Everyday Science

Water in Space?

All living things need water to survive. But Earth is the only planet we know about that has enough water to support life. Astrobiologists are scientists who study life in space. They're looking for planets outside the solar system that orbit a star. They want to see if there is water on these planets. If there is, there might be life on them too.

Scientists have identified more than 5,000 planets beyond our solar system. Planets that are too close to their star will be too hot. They won't have any liquid water. Planets that are too far from their star will be too cold. If there is water, it will be ice. If a planet is just the right distance from their star—in the Goldilocks zone—it might have liquid water, like Earth.

The James Webb Space Telescope launched in 2021. It is currently the largest telescope in space. Scientists use it to search for life on other planets.

Life on Mars

Scientists are looking for water in our solar system too. The Curiosity rover is a robot that landed on Mars in 2012. It collects soil samples for scientists to study.

Today the surface of the planet is dry and barren. By studying Mars, we have found that it probably had lakes, rivers, and even an ocean in the past.

Let's Experiment!

Make a Dam

Dams are amazing feats of engineering. They hold back water, storing huge amounts in a reservoir. When the water needs to be used, it can be released.

You will need:
- A large dish or plastic tub
- Modeling clay
- Craft sticks
- A jug of water

If you spill any water, clean it up quickly to avoid accidents.

1 Roll the modeling clay into small balls. Place the balls in a line down the middle of the dish. Stick the balls down firmly.

2 Add more balls along the top of the line until you reach the same height as the dish. Press the balls together tightly, so there are no gaps. You have made a wall.

3 Add craft sticks to both sides of the clay wall. Press the sticks into the wall firmly. This will make the wall strong.

4 Pour water into one side of the dish. The water should stay on that side. Congratulations! You have made a dam.

Note: if water fills both sides, try again. Carefully pour out the water. Add more clay balls or more craft sticks. Press the wall together firmly. Then repeat step 4.

THE HOOVER DAM

The Hoover Dam is on the Colorado River in the US. It is a hydroelectric dam. It uses water power to make electricity. Lake Mead is a reservoir formed by the dam.

Let's Experiment!

Sink or Swim?

Try this experiment to see whether things float better in fresh water (like lake or river water) or in salt water (like seawater).

You will need:
- An uncooked egg
- Water
- A large glass
- 4 tbsp (70 g) table salt

If you spill any water, clean it up quickly to avoid accidents.

1 Fill an empty glass with water. Carefully put an egg into the water.

2 Watch what happens.

3 Repeat the experiment but stir in the salt before you add the egg.

4 Add the egg and watch what happens. The egg in the salty water should float! If it doesn't, try again. This time, add more salt to the water.

WHY THINGS FLOAT

Salt water is denser than fresh water because it contains salt as well as water. Because of this extra density, objects (and animals!) float more easily in the ocean than in freshwater lakes and rivers. This baby eider is a sea duck. It spends a lot of time floating in salt water.

41

Vocabulary Builder
As the River Flows

There are many words we can use to describe the way that water moves. Read the story below to follow the journey of a stick from the start of a river to its end.

High in the mountains, a stream of water is formed by melting snow. A mountain goat passes and knocks a stick into the water. As the water flows down the mountain, it carries the stick along.

The stream flows into a pond. A frog hops on and off the stick. The stick keeps moving. More streams come together. A fast-flowing river is formed. The stick moves quickly, crashing over rocks and rapids. It spins past deep pools.

Along the riverbank, trees provide shade. An otter plays with the stick before letting go. As more streams and rivers come together, the water gets deeper and more powerful. The stick is almost lost in the huge river.

Near its end, the river gets broad and flat. The stick slowly flows past farmland and through a town. Finally, the river reaches the sea. The stick disappears in the waves, ready for new adventures.

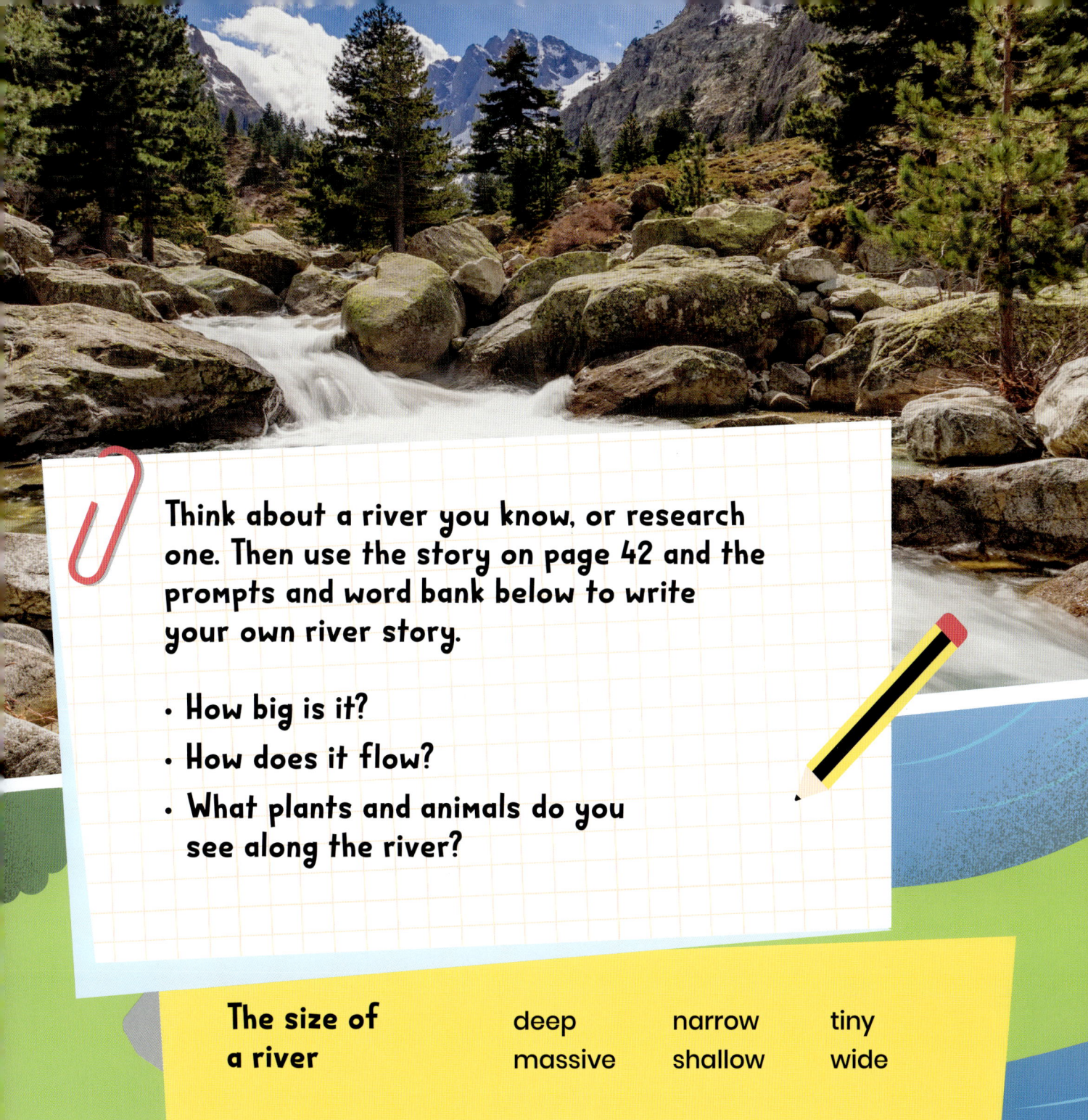

Think about a river you know, or research one. Then use the story on page 42 and the prompts and word bank below to write your own river story.

- How big is it?
- How does it flow?
- What plants and animals do you see along the river?

The size of a river	deep massive	narrow shallow	tiny wide
How a river flows	bubbling flooding	pouring rushing	splashing trickling
What lives by a river	dragonfly duck fish	geese insect reeds	tree turtle vole

Glossary

Atmosphere All the air that surrounds Earth.

Bay An indent where the ocean curves into the land.

Beach A broad, flat area that can be found next to oceans, rivers, or lakes.

Canal An artificial waterway connecting two bodies of water to allow boats to travel between them.

Civilization Any human society in the past or present that has culture and technology.

Cliff A high rock formation with a steep side.

Coast Where the land meets the sea.

Condensation The process in which water vapor in the air cools down and turns back into a liquid, forming tiny drops of water in clouds.

Current A flow of water that can be slow or fast, weak or strong.

Dam A structure built across a river that stores water in a reservoir and can be used to prevent flooding and generate electricity.

Divert To change the direction of something, such as a waterway.

Dock A structure built on a waterway that is used by people and boats.

Dune A hill of sand at the back of a beach. Dunes are formed by the wind.

Evaporation The process in which energy from the Sun causes liquid water in bodies of water to turn into water vapor, which then rises into the air and forms clouds.

Flood A flow of water onto dry land.

Flow To move in a stream.

Fresh water Water that is not salty and can be used as drinking water.

Glacier A huge mass of slow-moving ice.

Groundwater The water found below Earth's surface.

Gulf Part of the ocean that goes a long way into the land. Usually surrounded by land apart from one opening to the sea.

Habitat The natural home of a plant or animal.

Irrigation The watering of crops.

Lake A body of fresh water or salt water that is surrounded by land.

Lock A section of a canal that allows the water to be raised and lowered, which lifts and lowers boats that are traveling on the canal.

Mouth Where a river ends.

Ocean One of the large bodies of salt water that covers Earth.

Pasture A piece of land covered in grass and other plants that farm animals eat.

Precipitation The process in which the water droplets in clouds get so heavy that they fall back down to Earth as rain, snow, hail, or sleet.

Rapids A part of the river where the water moves very fast.

Reservoir An artificial lake that is formed behind a dam and stores water.

River A large stream of fresh water that flows into a body of water.

Riverbank One of the two sides of a river.

Runoff Liquid water that doesn't soak into the soil, but instead flows across the ground, forming streams and rivers.

Salt water Salty water that can not be used as drinking water.

Sea A large part of the ocean that is near land.

Source Where a river starts.

Strait A narrow passage that connects two seas.

Trading hub A central location for shipping and receiving goods around the world.

Transportation route A path that allows people to move goods or people from one location to another.

Tributary A small stream that flows into a river or lake.

Water vapor The gaseous state of water.

Index

A
Amazon 5, 33
animals, riverbank 20, 30–31
Aral Sea 17
Aswan Dam 25
Atacama Desert 4–5
Atlantic Ocean 19
atmosphere 8

B
bays 11
beaches 12–13
birds 14, 31
blood 7

C
Cairo 29
canals 19, 27
Cape Town 29
cliffs 12
climate change 12
coast 12
Colorado River 39
condensation 8
corals 10
Curiosity rover 37
currents 34–35

D
dams 17, 21, 24–25, 38–39
dangers 34–35
docks 14, 28
ducks 31, 41
dunes 12

E
Earth 5, 37
eider ducks 41
evaporation 8
experiments
　dams 38–39
　sink or swim? 40–41

F
farm ponds 28
farming 21, 22, 23, 28, 42
fish 10, 21, 31
floating experiment 40–41
floods 21, 24, 28, 35
flowing water story 42
frogs 20, 31

G
Ganges River 23
geese 31, 41
glaciers 5, 15
Great Lakes 18–19
Great Pacific Garbage Patch 11
groundwater 9, 14, 15
gulfs 11

H
habitats 30
hermit crabs 13
Hoover Dam 25, 39
Huáng Hé (Yellow River) 22
hurricanes 4

I
ice 7
insects 31
intake towers 24
invertebrates 10
irrigation 15, 20, 28

J
James Webb Space Telescope 36
Jawa Dam 24

K
Kariba Dam 25
kingfishers 31

L

Lake Baikal 17
Lake Chad 16
Lake Erie 19
Lake Huron 18
Lake Mead 39
Lake Michigan 18
Lake Ontario 19
Lake Superior 18
Lake Tanganyika 16
Lake Titicaca 17
Lake Victoria 17
lakes 4, 14–19
levees 28
living by the water 28–29
locks, canal 27

M

mangroves 31
maple syrup 7
Mars 37
Mississippi River 32, 34, 35
mouths, river 21
Murray River 23
mussels 13

N

navigation 35
New Orleans 29
Niagara Falls 27
Nile River 22, 25, 28, 33

O

Ob River 34
oceans 4–5, 10–11, 19

P

Pacific Ocean 5
paddle steamers 23
pastures 28
Phoenicians 33
planets 36–37
plasma 7
pollution 23, 33
pond skaters 31
ponds 9, 28, 31
Port of Manaus 33
ports 32, 33
power plants 20, 24–25, 39
precipitation 9

R

rainforests 5
rapids 34, 35
reefs 10
reservoirs 21, 24–25, 39
Rio Negro 33
rivers 20–23, 28, 32–33
runoff 9, 14

S

saltwater lakes 14, 15, 17
sea levels 5, 12
sea stars 10, 13
sea urchins 13
seas 11
seaweed 13
source of rivers 20
space 36–37
spillways 24
states of water 6–7
straits 11

T

terrapins 20
tide pools 12
trading places 32–33
transportation routes 32
trees 31
tributaries 21
trout 21

V

vapor, water 7, 8
Victoria Falls 27

W, Y

wastewater treatment plants 29
water 6–7
water cycle 8–9
water voles 31
waterfalls 26–27
waterside habitats 30–31
Welland Canal 27
wetlands 14, 20
whales 11
Yangtze River 34

Acknowledgments

The publisher would like to thank the following for their kind permission to reproduce their photographs:

(Key: a-above; b-below/bottom; c-center; f-far; l-left; r-right; t-top)

123RF.com: 25tr, Eric Isselee 5bc, tsuneo 11tl; **Alamy Stock Photo**: 21clb, Associated Press / Aloys Niyoyita 17br, blickwinkel / McPHOTO / MDF 16bl, Joerg Boethling 33br, Tosh Brown 31tl, Connect Images / Gu 22tr, CueImages 7tr, DanitaDelimont / Gayle Harper 35tr, Reinhard Dirscherl 29tr, Geopix 37r, Robert Henno 13tc, Mark Hicken 41br, Cindy Hopkins 19br, imageBROKER.com GmbH & Co. KG / Gerhard Zwerger-Schoner 13tl, Gre Jak 37cl, frans lemmens 6-7tc, Fir Mamat 13ca, Melba Photo Agency 17cla, Stephen Barnes / Military 35crb, Nature Picture Library / Bernard Castelein 15crb, Kasia Nowak 16crb, Ingo Oeland 23bl, Panoramic Images 26-27, Gavin Thorn 30b, Xinhua / Huang Wei 34cra; **Depositphotos Inc**: 2630ben 27cla, alenka2194 35tl, kandinskiy_ 25br; **Dorling Kindersley**: Thomas Marent 31cr; **Dreamstime.com**: Bennymarty 15tl, Mikhail Blajenov 13bc, Dvrcan 17cra, Eagle 31cl, Vlad Ghiea 18br, Vitalii Hryshko 31bl, Jaysi 18clb, Joningall 43t, Kharlamova 33tr, Rachapol Kitjanukit 14cr, Sergii Kolesnyk 22bl, Andrey Koturanov 21cla, Iuliia Kuzenkova 16tr, Paul Lemke / Lokinthru 18tr, Martin Maritz 30br, William Morgan 32tr, Susan Robinson / Suerob 31bc, Prasit Rodphan / Ake1150sb 32bc, Seadam 10bc, Skornstein3 13br, Kenneth Sponsler 19clb, Bidouze Stephane 4-5b, Vanja Terzic 39br, Kelly Vandellen 35cb, Oksana Vinopalova 25cr, Wrangel 13cra, Rudmer Zwerver 31br; **ESA**: NASA, ESA, CSA, and STScI, J. DePasquale (STScI) 36-37; **Fotolia**: Nataly-Nete 20bc; **Getty Images**: Emad aljumah 6b, grandriver 29br; **Getty Images / iStock**: AndreaWillmore 29cr, drakuliren 30tr, E+ / Sportstock 27clb, JanMiko 31tr, johnny123 15tr, mbala mbala merlin 11bl, PurpleImages 31tc; **Shutterstock.com**: CherylRamalho 23ca, SofotoCool 7br

Cover images: *Front*: **Getty Images / iStock**: Aleksandr Durnov b, epic_fail tl, Olha Furmaniuk tr, oleg7799 bl, Seamartini cb, Akkachai Thothubthai t; **Shutterstock.com**: Nostagrams br; *Back*: **Dreamstime.com**: Sergii Kolesnyk cl, Rudmer Zwerver tl